CATHLEEN NI HOULIHAN

By W. B. YEATS

A Digireads.com Book
Digireads.com Publishing

Cathleen Ni Houlihan
By W. B. Yeats
ISBN 10: 1-4209-4157-7
ISBN 13: 978-1-4209-4157-9

Please visit *www.digireads.com*

PERSONS IN THE PLAY

PETER GILLANE
MICHAEL GILLANE, his son, going to be married.
PATRICK GILLANE, a lad of twelve, Michael's brother.
BRIDGET GILLANE, Peter's wife.
DELIA CAHEL, engaged to MICHAEL.
THE POOR OLD WOMAN
NEIGHBOURS

> [*Interior of a cottage close to Killala, in 1798. Bridget is standing at a table undoing a parcel. Peter is sitting at one side of the fire, Patrick at the other.*]

PETER. What is that sound I hear?

PATRICK. I don't hear anything. [*He listens.*] I hear it now. It's like cheering. [*He goes to the window and looks out.*] I wonder what they are cheering about. I don't see anybody.

PETER. It might be a hurling match.

PATRICK. There's no hurling to-day. It must be down in the town the cheering is.

BRIDGET. I suppose the boys must be having some sport of their own. Come over here, Peter, and look at Michael's wedding-clothes.

PETER. [*shifts his chair to table*] Those are grand clothes, indeed.

BRIDGET. You hadn't clothes like that when you married me, and no coat to put on of a Sunday any more than any other day.

PETER. That is true, indeed. We never thought a son of our own would be wearing a suit of that sort for his wedding, or have so good a place to bring a wife to.

PATRICK. [*who is still at the window*] There's an old woman coming down the road. I don't know, is it here she's coming?

BRIDGET. It will be a neighbour coming to hear about Michael's wedding. Can you see who it is?

PATRICK. I think it is a stranger, but she's not coming to the house. She's turned into the gap that goes down where Maurteen and his sons are shearing sheep. [*He turns towards Bridget.*] Do you remember what Winny of the Cross Roads was saying the other night about the strange woman that goes through the country whatever time there's war or trouble coming?

BRIDGET. Don't be bothering us about Winny's talk, but go and open the door for your brother. I hear him coming up the path.

PETER. I hope he has brought Delia's fortune with him safe, for fear her people might go back on the bargain and I after making it. Trouble enough I had making it.

[*Patrick opens the door and Michael comes in.*]

BRIDGET. What kept you, Michael? We were looking out for you this long time.

MICHAEL. I went round by the priest's house to bid him be ready to marry us to-morrow.

BRIDGET. Did he say anything?

MICHAEL. He said it was a very nice match, and that he was never better pleased to marry any two in his parish than myself and Delia Cahel.

PETER. Have you got the fortune, Michael?

MICHAEL. Here it is.

[*Michael puts bag on table and goes over and leans against the chimney-jamb. Bridget, who has been all this time examining the clothes, pulling the seams and trying the lining of the pockets, etc., puts the clothes on the dresser.*]

PETER. [*getting up and taking the bag in his hand and turning out the money*] Yes, I made the bargain well for you, Michael. Old John Cahel would sooner have kept a share of this awhile longer. "Let me keep the half of it till the first boy is born," says he. "You will not," says I. "Whether there is or is not a boy, the whole hundred pounds must be in Michael's hands before he brings your daughter in the house." The wife spoke to him then, and he gave in at the end.

BRIDGET. You seem well pleased to be handling the money, Peter.

PETER. Indeed, I wish I had had the luck to get a hundred pounds, or twenty pounds itself, with the wife I married.

BRIDGET. Well, if I didn't bring much I didn't get much. What had you the day I married you but a flock of hens and you feeding them, and a few lambs and you driving them to the market at Ballina? [*She is vexed and bangs a jug on the dresser.*] If I brought no fortune, I worked it out in my bones, laying down the baby, Michael that is standing there now, on a stook of straw, while I dug the potatoes, and never asking big dresses or anything but to be working.

PETER. That is true, indeed. [*He pats her arm.*]

BRIDGET. Leave me alone now till I ready the house for the woman that is to come into it.

PETER. You are the best woman in Ireland, but money is good, too. [*He begins handling the money again and sits down.*] I never thought to see so much money within my four walls. We can do great things now we have it. We can take the ten acres of land we have a chance of since Jamsie Dempsey died, and stock it. We will go to the fair of Ballina to buy the stock. Did Delia ask any of the money for her own use, Michael?

MICHAEL. She did not, indeed. She did not seem to take much notice of it, or to look at it at all.

BRIDGET. That's no wonder. Why would she look at it when she had yourself to look at, a fine, strong young man? It is proud she must be to get you, a good steady boy that will make use of the money, and not be running through it or spending it on drink like another.

PETER. It's likely Michael himself was not thinking much of the fortune either, but of what sort the girl was to look at.

MICHAEL. [*coming over towards the table*] Well, you would like a nice comely girl to be beside you, and to go walking with you. The fortune only lasts for a while, but the woman will be there always.

PATRICK. [*turning round from the window*] They are cheering again down in the town. Maybe they are landing horses from Enniscrone. They do be cheering when the horses take the water well.

MICHAEL. There are no horses in it. Where would they be going and no fair at hand? Go down to the town, Patrick, and see what is going on.

PATRICK. [*opens the door to go out, but stops for a moment on the threshold*] Will Delia remember, do you think, to bring the greyhound pup she promised me when she would be coming to the house?

MICHAEL. She will surely.

[*Patrick goes out, leaving the door open.*]

PETER. It will be Patrick's turn next to be looking for a fortune, but he won't find it so easy to get it and he with no place of his own.

BRIDGET. I do be thinking sometimes, now things are going so well with us, and the Cahels such a good back to us in the district, and Delia's own uncle a priest, we might be put in the way of making Patrick a priest some day, and he so good at his books.

PETER. Time enough, time enough; you have always your head full of plans, Bridget.

BRIDGET. We will be well able to give him learning, and not to send him trampling the country like a poor scholar that lives on charity.

MICHAEL. They're not done cheering yet.

[*He goes over to the door and stands there for a moment, putting up his hand to shade his eyes.*]

BRIDGET. Do you see anything?

MICHAEL. I see an old woman coming up the path.

BRIDGET. Who is it, I wonder. It must be the strange woman Patrick saw awhile ago.

MICHAEL. I don't think it's one of the neighbours anyway, but she has her cloak over her face.

BRIDGET. It might be some poor woman heard we were making ready for the wedding and came to look for her share.

PETER. I may as well put the money out of sight. There is no use leaving it out for every stranger to look at.

[*He goes over to a large box in the corner, opens it, and puts the bag in and fumbles at the lock.*]

MICHAEL. There she is, father! [*An Old Woman passes the window slowly; she looks at Michael as she passes.*] I'd sooner a stranger not to come to the house the night before my wedding.

BRIDGET. Open the door, Michael; don't keep the poor woman waiting.

[*The Old Woman comes in. Michael stands aside to make way for her.*]

OLD WOMEN. God save all here!

PETER. God save you kindly!

OLD WOMEN. You have good shelter here.

PETER. You are welcome to whatever shelter we have.

BRIDGET. Sit down there by the fire and welcome.

OLD WOMEN. [*warming her hands*] There is a hard wind outside.

[*Michael watches her curiously from the door. Peter comes over to the table.*]

PETER. Have you travelled far to-day?

OLD WOMEN. I have travelled far, very far; there are few have travelled so far as myself, and there's many a one that doesn't make me welcome. There was one that had strong sons I thought were friends of mine, but they were shearing their sheep, and they wouldn't listen to me.

PETER. It's a pity indeed for any person to have no place of their own.

OLD WOMEN. That's true for you indeed, and it's long I'm on the roads since I first went wandering.

BRIDGET. It is a wonder you are not worn out with so much wandering.

OLD WOMEN. Sometimes my feet are tired and my hands are quiet, but there is no quiet in my heart. When the people see me quiet, they think old age has come on me and that all the stir has gone out of me. But when the trouble is on me I must be talking to my friends.

BRIDGET. What was it put you wandering?

OLD WOMEN. Too many strangers in the house.

BRIDGET. Indeed you look as if you'd had your share of trouble.

OLD WOMEN. I have had trouble indeed.

BRIDGET. What was it put the trouble on you?

OLD WOMEN. My land that was taken from me.

PETER. Was it much land they took from you?

OLD WOMEN. My four beautiful green fields.

PETER. [*aside to Bridget*] Do you think could she be the widow Casey that was put out of her holding at Kilglass awhile ago?

BRIDGET. She is not. I saw the widow Casey one time at the market in Ballina, a stout fresh woman.

PETER. [*to Old Woman*] Did you hear a noise of cheering, and you coming up the hill?

OLD WOMEN. I thought I heard the noise I used to hear when my friends came to visit me.

[*She begins singing half to herself.*]

I will go cry with the woman,
For yellow-haired Donough is dead,
With a hempen rope for a neckcloth,
And a white cloth on his head,—

MICHAEL. [*coming from the door*] What is that you are singing, ma'am?

OLD WOMEN. Singing I am about a man I knew one time, yellow-haired Donough, that was hanged in Galway. [*She goes on singing, much louder*.]

> I am come to cry with you, woman,
> My hair is unwound and unbound;
> I remember him ploughing his field,
> Turning up the red side of the ground,
> And building his barn on the hill
> With the good mortared stone;
> O! we'd have pulled down the gallows
> Had it happened in Enniscrone!

MICHAEL. What was it brought him to his death?

OLD WOMEN. He died for love of me: many a man has died for love of me.

PETER. [*aside to Bridget*] Her trouble has put her wits astray.

MICHAEL. Is it long since that song was made? Is it long since he got his death?

OLD WOMEN. Not long, not long. But there were others that died for love of me a long time ago.

MICHAEL. Were they neighbours of your own, ma'am?

OLD WOMEN. Come here beside me and I'll tell you about them. [*Michael sits down beside her at the hearth.*] There was a red man of the O'Donnells from the north, and a man of the O'Sullivans from the south, and there was one Brian that lost his life at Clontarf by the sea, and there were a great many in the west, some that died hundreds of years ago, and there are some that will die to-morrow.

MICHAEL. Is it in the west that men will die to-morrow?

OLD WOMEN. Come nearer, nearer to me.

BRIDGET. Is she right, do you think? Or is she a woman from beyond the world?

PETER. She doesn't know well what she's talking about, with the want and the trouble she has gone through.

BRIDGET. The poor thing, we should treat her well.

PETER. Give her a drink of milk and a bit of the oaten cake.

BRIDGET. Maybe we should give her something along with that, to bring her on her way. A few pence, or a shilling itself, and we with so much money in the house.

PETER. Indeed I'd not begrudge it to her if we had it to spare, but if we go running through what we have, we'll soon have to break the hundred pounds, and that would be a pity.

BRIDGET. Shame on you, Peter. Give her the shilling, and your blessing with it, or our own luck will go from us.

[*Peter goes to the box and takes out a shilling.*]

BRIDGET. [*to the Old Woman*] Will you have a drink of milk?

OLD WOMEN. It is not food or drink that I want.

PETER. [*offering the shilling*] Here is something for you.

OLD WOMEN. That is not what I want. It is not silver I want.

PETER. What is it you would be asking for?

OLD WOMEN. If anyone would give me help he must give me himself, he must give me all.

[*Peter goes over to the table, staring at the shilling in his hand in a bewildered way, and stands whispering to Bridget.*]

MICHAEL. Have you no one to care you in your age, ma'am?

OLD WOMEN. I have not. With all the lovers that brought me their love, I never set out the bed for any.

MICHAEL. Are you lonely going the roads, ma'am?

OLD WOMEN. I have my thoughts and I have my hopes.

MICHAEL. What hopes have you to hold to?

OLD WOMEN. The hope of getting my beautiful fields back again; the hope of putting the strangers out of my house.

MICHAEL. What way will you do that, ma'am?

OLD WOMEN. I have good friends that will help me. They are gathering to help me now. I am not afraid. If they are put down to-day, they will get the upper hand to-morrow. [*She gets up.*] I must be going to meet my friends. They are coming to help me, and I must be there to welcome them. I must call the neighbours together to welcome them.

MICHAEL. I will go with you.

BRIDGET. It is not her friends you have to go and welcome, Michael; it is the girl coming into the house you have to welcome. You have plenty to do, it is food and drink you have to bring to the house. The woman that is coming home is not coming with empty hands; you would not have an empty house before her. [*To the Old Woman.*] Maybe you don't know, ma'am, that my son is going to be married to-morrow.

OLD WOMEN. It is not a man going to his marriage that I look to for help.

PETER. [*to Bridget*] Who is she, do you think, at all?

BRIDGET. You did not tell us your name yet, ma'am.

OLD WOMEN. Some call me the Poor Old Woman, and there are some that call me Cathleen, the daughter of Houlihan.

PETER. I think I knew someone of that name once. Who was it, I wonder? It must have been someone I knew when I was a boy. No, no, I remember, I heard it in a song.

OLD WOMEN. [*who is standing in the doorway*] They are wondering that there were songs made for me; there have been many songs made for me. I heard one on the wind this morning. [*She sings.*]

> Do not make a great keening
> When the graves have been dug to-morrow.
> Do not call the white-scarfed riders
> To the burying that shall be to-morrow.
>
> Do not spread food to call strangers
> To the wakes that shall be to-morrow;
> Do not give money for prayers
> For the dead that shall die to-morrow ...

They will have no need of prayers, they will have no need of prayers.

MICHAEL. I do not know what that song means, but tell me something I can do for you.

PETER. Come over to me, Michael.

MICHAEL. Hush, father, listen to her.

OLD WOMEN. It is a hard service they take that help me. Many that are red-cheeked now will be pale-cheeked; many that have been free to walk the hills and the bogs and the rushes will be sent to walk hard streets in far countries; many a good plan will be broken; many that have gathered money will not stay to spend it; many a child will be born, and there will be no father at its christening to give it a name. They that had red cheeks will have pale cheeks for my sake; and for all that, they will think they are well paid.

[*She goes out; her voice is heard outside singing.*]

> They shall be remembered for ever,
> They shall be alive for ever,
> They shall be speaking for ever,
> The people shall hear them for ever.

BRIDGET. [*to Peter*] Look at him, Peter; he has the look of a man that has got the touch. [*Raising her voice.*] Look here, Michael, at the wedding-clothes. Such grand clothes as these are. You have a right to fit them on now; it would be a pity to-morrow if they did not fit. The boys would be laughing at you. Take them, Michael, and go into the room and fit them on. [*She puts them on his arm.*]

MICHAEL. What wedding are you talking of? What clothes will I be wearing to-morrow?

BRIDGET. These are the clothes you are going to wear when you marry Delia Cahel to-morrow.

MICHAEL. I had forgotten that.

[*He looks at the clothes and turns towards the inner room, but stops at the sound of cheering outside.*]

PETER. There is the shouting come to our own door. What is it has happened?

[*Neighbours come crowding in, Patrick and Delia with them.*]

PATRICK. There are ships in the Bay; the French are landing at Killala!

[*Peter takes his pipe from his mouth and his hat off, and stands up. The clothes slip from Michael's arm.*]

DELIA. Michael! [*He takes no notice.*] Michael! [*He turns towards her.*] Why do you look at me like a stranger?

[*She drops his arm. Bridget goes over towards her.*]

PATRICK. The boys are all hurrying down the hillsides to join the French.

DELIA. Michael won't be going to join the French.

BRIDGET. [*to Peter*] Tell him not to go, Peter.

PETER. It's no use. He doesn't hear a word we're saying.

BRIDGET. Try and coax him over to the fire.

DELIA. Michael! Michael! You won't leave me! You won't join the French, and we going to be married!

[*She puts her arms about him; he turns towards her as if about to yield. Old Woman's voice outside.*]

They shall be speaking for ever, The people shall hear them for ever.

[*Michael breaks away from Delia and goes out.*]

PETER. [*to Patrick, laying a hand on his arm*] Did you see an old woman going down the path?

PATRICK. I did not, but I saw a young girl, and she had the walk of a queen.

THE END

CPSIA information can be obtained
at www.ICGtesting.com
Printed in the USA
LVHW101915080922
727888LV00004B/606